SCOTLAND'S KING OF FISH

Derek Mills

WILLIAM BLACKWOOD
1980

First published in 1980 by
William Blackwood & Sons Ltd
32 Thistle Street
Edinburgh EH2 1HA
Scotland

ISBN 0 85158 134 X

Printed at the Press of
the Publisher

Contents

Illustrations

'*The salmon is accounted the king of freshwater fish, and is ever bred in rivers relating to the sea* . . .'

Izaak Walton, 1653

Introduction

The salmon gray of Tweed or Spey,
Returning from the sea,
Seeks to its native river stream,
Whichever stream it be.
Even spirits 'mong celestial orbs,
In glory roaming free,
May owe to earth, their first abode,
A soul-felt sympathy.

THIS verse, written by John Younger, a St Boswells shoemaker, in 1837, echoed my own feelings on returning to Scotland from Canada in the late 1950s to take up a professional appointment with a salmon-research project in Ross-shire. I had started my career as a marine biologist in Aberdeen and therefore had a fellow feeling for the salmon and could appreciate its life out in the storm-swept Arctic seas.

I have seen and handled countless salmon since the 1950s but still look on them with admiration, and marvel at the way they return from distant feeding-grounds to their river of origin.

In 1959 Arthur Ransome said in the preface to his book *Mainly About Fishing*: 'When the little fish leave the rivers and go to sea, the fisherman loses touch with them altogether. . . . They disappear behind a seemingly impenetrable curtain. We do not know for certain whither they go, though it does at least seem that we may be on the point of finding out.'

Alas, we have found out and we are none the better for it. Man's greed is getting the better of him and our salmon are now being taken on their feeding-grounds. It is the fervent

1

desire of all of us concerned with salmon conservation to see that reason prevails, otherwise there will be no more 'salmon gray' returning to the Tweed or Spey, or to any other river for that matter.

The Atlantic Salmon

THE Atlantic salmon (*Salmo salar*) is a migratory fish found in the temperate and Arctic regions of the northern hemisphere. It is referred to as being anadromous because of its habit of migrating from the sea into fresh water to spawn. This is the exact opposite of the common eel which leaves the rivers to spawn in the Sargasso Sea and is therefore catadromous.

At the present time the salmon is found in more than 200 rivers in Scotland, and that does not include any of the small coastal streams which it may frequent for only a short time before spawning.

There are few fish, other than the closely related Pacific salmon, which have such a fascinating life-cycle. The salmon uses the gravel in the streams and rivers for the protection of its eggs and the fresh waters themselves for the nursery stage of its life. Then in the spring of the year, when the young fish are a few inches long and able to cope with conditions at sea, they leave the rivers in their thousands to feed voraciously; they grow to a weight of several pounds in a time which they had taken to make only a few ounces when in the river. There is no more handsome a fish than the salmon, with the blue and silver of its body reflecting the very colours of the ocean where it feeds on small fish and plankton and stores the goodness of this rich larder in the form of the deep-red flesh which makes it such a prized quarry.

There are a number of countries, although not Scotland, in which some of the Atlantic Salmon never go to sea, and they are referred to as 'landlocked' salmon. In some cases this modified life-cycle has been caused by the salmon's access to the sea being barred. In Lake Vänern in Sweden there is such a non-migratory form of Atlantic salmon called 'blanklax'. This salmon enters the rivers running into the lake to breed, and the smolts migrate to the lake where they live until it is time for them to return to the rivers to spawn. Landlocked salmon also occur in Russia, in Lake Ladoga. However, in several lakes in eastern North America there is a form of landlocked salmon, known in Quebec as *Ouananiche*, where access to the sea is not barred. This is the situation, too, in South Island, New Zealand, where the majority of the salmon, many of Scottish origin, in the streams running into Lake Te Anau descend only to this lake and, after feeding there for a number of months, return to the headwaters to spawn.

The Atlantic salmon can grow to a very large size and the biggest are usually caught in Norwegian rivers. However, some very large ones have been recorded in Scottish waters. It is generally accepted that the largest one caught on rod and line in Scotland weighed 64 lb and was taken from the River Tay by Miss G. Ballantyne in 1922. However, the 8th Earl of Home is recorded as having caught a 69¾-lb specimen in the River Tweed in 1730, and a famous poacher named Jock Wallace landed a fish of 67 lb at Barjog on the Nith in 1812. This fish was hooked about eight in the morning and landed at six in the evening, by which time, it is reported, only two strands of Jock's hair line held the fish. Frank Buckland, a past Inspector of Salmon Fisheries in England and Wales, describes in his book *The Natural History of British Fishes* (1891) a monster salmon of 70 lb taken from the Tay. The fish had been caught in the nets of his friend Mr Alexander Speedie on the Haggis fishing-bank, about two miles below Newburgh. The total length of the fish was 4 ft 5 in., its girth 2 ft 7½ in. and length of head 12 in. The fish was painted to life by the well-known artist H. L. Rolfe.

The salmon which I am sure we would all like to consider the largest caught is something of a mystery, but it is said to have weighed 103 lb. If we accept the opinion of Mr W. L. Calderwood, one-time Inspector of Salmon Fisheries for Scotland, then this fish holds the record; but let Mr Calderwood tell the story in his own words:

4

18 lb female salmon and 49½ lb male salmon caught on the rod in the Tay

Female Salmon 18lbs

'It was at the mouth of the Devon [a tributary of the Forth] that, during the winter of 1901 or 1902, three fishermen, who were not particularly anxious to have their movements observed, are reported to have caught a salmon of 103 lb. No visible record of this monster was retained, so that no actual proof can be produced. On this account it is not surprising that many decline to believe in the fish's existence. I had, however, an opportunity of putting questions to one of the men, and as a result I accepted the statement he made, viz, that the fish weighed 103 lb and a few ounces.'

The salmon has a number of near relations which also frequent Scottish waters; these include the sea trout, brown trout, char, powan, vendace and grayling. They all bear the hallmark of the salmon family in the form of the little fatty adipose fin which has no fin rays and is situated on the back close to the tail.

The sea trout and brown trout are the same species—*Salmo trutta*. The sea trout is simply a brown trout which is migratory and goes to sea in the spring of the year as a smolt where it feeds and grows to a larger size than it would had it remained for a similar time in fresh water. Unlike the salmon it does not travel great distances while at sea and may return to the river a number of years in succession to spawn.

The brown trout is 'the country cousin' and occurs in various colours and sizes in every clean burn, stream, river, lochan and loch in Scotland, and is the mainstay of Scottish angling.

The trout is much stockier in shape than a salmon and has a much squarer tail (see page 7). A simple method of distinguishing a salmon from a sea trout, but one with which a taxonomist would not agree, lies in the fact that you can grasp a salmon by its tail because of the well-defined 'wrist' in front of the firm tail fin, but on picking up a sea trout by the wrist of the tail it slips through your fingers due to the tail fin folding up and not providing a firm grip. To be more

Salmon (top) and sea trout (bottom)

precise, a salmon usually has eleven scales running from the posterior edge of the adipose fin downwards and forwards to the lateral line, whereas the trout usually has fourteen; and there are usually eleven rays in the dorsal fin of the salmon and nine in that of the trout.

The char (sometimes spelt charr) is an Arctic fish which in Scotland dwells mainly in the deep cold lochs of the north. It is a pretty fish, particularly at spawning time when its belly is bright red, contrasting sharply with its black back and the white stripes on its fins. In the more northerly Arctic areas the char frequents rivers as well and has a migratory and non-migratory form, the migratory form going to sea in the summer but returning to fresh water to spawn. James Ritchie in his fascinating book *The Influences of Man on Animal Life in Scotland* (Cambridge University Press, 1920) refers to the enormous number of char in Loch Insh near Aviemore in Inverness-shire, which were caught as they moved into the River Spey to spawn. The fish were either netted or snared with a simple ring of brass at the end of a long stick. The fish were pickled with salt and preserved for winter use. Alas the char are no longer so plentiful in Loch Insh, which is perhaps not surprising.

The char was always thought to be associated with the large brown trout referred to as the 'ferox' trout. These very heavy fish, weighing into double figures, are heavily marked with large black spots merging dorsally and extending to cover almost the entire flanks of the fish, over a background of deep gold. Niall Campbell of the Nature Conservancy Council recently made an exhaustive survey of char and ferox trout lochs in Scotland and found that of eighty-eight lochs containing char, fifty-seven of them also contain ferox trout and thirty-seven of those containing ferox were over 200 ha. in area.

The powan and vendace are what are known as whitefish, or coregonids, and are herring-like in appearance. These two are the only species which occur in Scotland although they and other species occur in great abundance in Scandinavia, Eastern Europe and Canada. The powan is confined to Loch

Lomond and Loch Eck, and the vendace to Mill Loch near Lochmaben in Dumfriesshire. It was said that the vendace was introduced to this loch by Mary, Queen of Scots. The vendace was considered a great delicacy and there were two angling clubs devoted to its capture, one for the 'gentry' and the other for working folk. The latter club at times had as many as 2,000 members.

The grayling is 'on the fringe', one might say, and in some parts of the country is considered strictly non-U; but just as the chambermaid can tickle his lordship's fancy so can the grayling provide delightful sport for the salmon and trout angler during the winter months when it is at its best. The grayling is a very becoming fish being silvery-grey in colour, with a few black spots on its flanks, and possessing an exceptionally large red and black, almost fan-like dorsal fin. When you take it out of your landing net—with frost-bitten hands—it actually smells of cucumber. The grayling frequents only the rivers in the south of Scotland and is not found farther north than the River Tummel at Pitlochry. Its chief haunts are the rivers Earn, Isla, Tweed, Teviot, Clyde and Nith. It is almost certain that it was introduced to Scotland. This is borne out in the dedication by William Brown to his book *The Natural History of the Salmon as Ascertained by the Recent Experiments in the Artificial Spawning and Hatching of the Ova and Rearing of the Fry, at Stormontfeld, on the Tay* (1862), which reads:

'To the Members and Honorary Members of The West of Scotland Angling Club Who First Introduced the Grayling to Scotland, and have been successful in its Artificial Propagation in the Clyde. . . .'

A grayling society has recently been formed which should guarantee the fish a respectable reputation in the future. But let us return to the salmon.

The Life Story

IT may seem strange that adult salmon should stop feeding and enter the rivers of their birth from January onwards when they are not going to spawn until the late autumn. It could be argued that if they were to remain in the sea for a few more months and continue devouring sand eels, herring and sprats they would add a few more pounds to their weight and return closer to their time of spawning, thus reducing the time in which they are vulnerable to the hazards of netting, poaching, angling and disease. However, nature has it otherwise and very sensibly too. If all our salmon were to return at the same time, and drought, pollution or disease were to occur, the whole year's spawning stock could perish; and of course the netting and rod-fishing activity would be concentrated into a short period rather than extending from mid-January to the end of November. It is this pattern of behaviour which makes the salmon such a valuable natural asset upon which a viable industry is based.

Salmon returning to their river of origin in the early months of the year after spending two or more years at sea are referred to as 'spring fish'. They are the basis of the spring salmon rod-fishing for which so many Scottish rivers are renowned. Though how anyone can refer to a fish returning to the river in late December or early January, or even February for that matter, as a 'spring' fish is beyond comprehension; and when angling on the Tay, the Aberdeenshire Dee and the Tweed in January and February in arctic conditions of snow and ice, with frequent resort to the national beverage, is referred to as 'spring fishing', then those that are not followers of the gentle art must shake their heads in disbelief. However, spring fishing it is, and these early fish are spring fish, as are their colleagues ascending at the more seasonable times of April and early May.

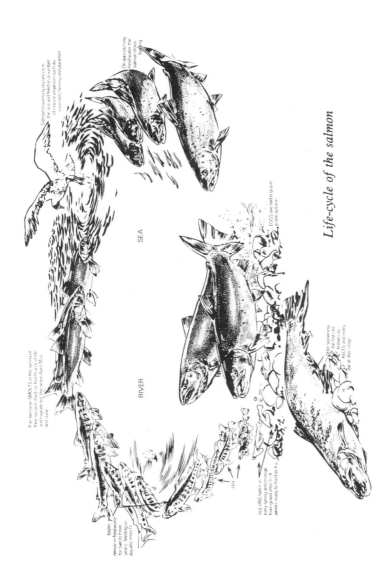

Life-cycle of the salmon

Salmon travel long distances in the sea and feed on a number of marine organisms such as sandeels, herrings and plankton

On approaching freshwater the salmon stops feeding

EGGS are laid in gravel in late autumn

After spawning the fish are known as KELTS and many die at this stage

SEA

RIVER

Parr become SMOLTS in the spring of their second, third, or fourth year of life and migrate to the sea in April, May and June

PARR remain in freshwater for two to three years, feeding on aquatic insects

ALEVINS hatch in early spring and emerge from gravel after 3–4 weeks, ready to feed as fry

FRY

By late May the run of summer fish begins with fish that have dwelt for more than two or three years at sea, and then, by mid-June, the first of the younger fish start to ascend. The latter, having spent only a little over a year at sea, are referred to as 'grilse' (from the Norse *grålax*—grey salmon). The commercial salmon fishermen tend to refer to any summer fish under 7 or 8 lb as being a grilse and fish over that weight as a salmon. However, many grilse caught by anglers fishing the Tweed in October and November weigh upwards of that weight, with fish of 11 to 12 lb being recorded frequently.

Some rivers such as the Tweed, Annan and Nith have a run of 'late', or 'autumn', fish in October and November. These tend to be large, weighing well into double figures, with some exceeding 30 lb. In the rivers of south-west Scotland these fish are referred to as 'greybacks', a rather loose term covering any large late-running salmon.

It is not every salmon river in Scotland that can boast runs of salmon throughout the year. Our bigger rivers, the Tay, Tweed and Spey, can, although only the Tweed has the very late run for which it is famed. On the west coast of Scotland and in the Western Isles salmon enter fresh water from about the end of June to October, although there are exceptions, and the Skealtar system in North Uist has a number of salmon appearing in February and March.

The time at which fish enter a river may change over the years; no river has shown this more clearly than the Tweed, where over the last 100 years there has been a complete cycle. In the 1880s and '90s autumn fish predominated, but gradually the proportions of autumn and spring fish in the rod catches changed, so that by the 1930s spring fish were the most abundant. Then in the late 1960s a marked decline in the number of spring fish became apparent and autumn fish began to reappear in increasing numbers. The decline in the runs of spring fish in recent years has been common to many Scottish rivers, and in most there has been a tendency for salmon to appear later in the year than in the previous decade. This is not to say that spring fish are absent from many of these rivers; the Spey, Tay and Tweed still have spring runs, and the northern Sutherland rivers such as the Brora, Cassley, Helmsdale and Naver still provide excellent spring fishing. But the glorious years of spring fishing are memories of the past.

No one can say for sure why there has been a change in the time of entry of adult fish. Some believe that the hydro-electric developments on many of the major Scottish rivers have both influenced the behaviour of returning adults and destroyed the spawning areas of the spring fish. On rivers unaffected by hydro-electric schemes it is suggested that the late-running fish, entering as they do after the netting season is over, predominate and compete successfully with the springers for the available spawning areas. Until such time as we can collect and examine, with the aid of a computer, data on climate, river flows, ocean currents and salmon catches, we shall have to continue to speculate and allow our 'experts' full rein.

Much of our knowledge of salmon stocks has relied on the fact that we can use the scales of a salmon to tell its age and past history. The concentric rings of the scales, like the cross-section of the trunk of a tree, can reveal the age of the fish. When the young salmon first emerges from the gravel it has no scales, but very soon papillae start to appear along each side and develop quickly into small calcareous plates which, as they grow, lay down rings, or 'circuli' at regular intervals. During periods of rapid growth occurring in the warmer months when fish are feeding more actively, the rings are widely spaced, but during the winter months, when feeding activity is reduced, the circuli are laid down close together, giving the appearance under the microscope of a dark band, known as an 'annulus'. The annulus is complete by the end of the period of little or no feeding in the winter. Once feeding recommences in the late spring, the circuli are again more widely spaced. So, by counting the number of annuli, or winter bands, the age of the fish can be determined. Much more information can be gleaned from scales. It is possible by microscopical examination to estimate the

13

length of the fish at the end of each year of its life, because the scale grows in direct proportion to the length of the fish.

A Scotsman, H. W. Johnston, was the first to discover that the age of the salmon could be obtained from an examination of its scales. His findings were published in *The Field* in 1904 and later in the Annual Reports of the Fishery Board for Scotland. A scale is therefore a very useful identity card and provides the biologist with the information from which it is possible to build up a complete story of the stocks of salmon in our rivers. Early Scottish salmon biologists such as Calderwood, Malloch, Menzies and Nall did much of the pioneer work in this field, helped by Johnston's earlier work.

It is said that adult salmon do not feed in fresh water, but it is not easy to explain why this is so when it is common knowledge that they are caught by anglers using artificial flies and minnows and fresh garden worms. The usual reply is that it is nature's way of insuring that the young salmon are not all devoured by their older relatives, and that it is only curiosity or anger, or the recurrence of a lost feeding stimulus, which triggers off the taking of an angler's lure.

It is said that the stomach becomes occluded and will not accept food, but a salmon caught on a worm has invariably swallowed it. However, a reduced flow of digestive juices to the stomach on return to fresh water would severely restrict the type of organism that could be digested, and probably the salmon is therefore able to squash only the soft-bodied organisms and so digest the minimum quantity of food. The actual point in its return migration at which food intake is reduced is not known. Salmon taken in the coastal nets frequently have their stomachs full of sand eels, and it is worth noting that the occasional young salmon has been found in the stomach of an adult in the river. In 1894 and 1895 a gentleman named Tosh examined the contents of 1,694 salmon from the River Tweed. Some of the fish (1,142) were caught in the estuary and others (252) were taken some thirty miles upstream near Kelso. Just under 10 per cent of those fish taken in the estuary contained recognisable food, much of it marine in origin, but all the stomachs from the Kelso fish were empty. However, a study of the cellular activity of the stomach and intestine of the salmon would be most rewarding, and perhaps it might confirm or disprove the theory presented by Eric Linklater in his pamphlet *The Secret Larder or How a Salmon Lives and Why it Dies* (1969), which propounds that the minute particles of decaying flesh from the carcasses of kelts and diseased fish provide a semi-digested form of food suitable for the shrunken stomach of the returning fish.

The explanation provided by Arthur Ransome in *Mainly About Fishing* is the most fascinating of all. The idea came to him while watching American soldiers chewing gum in the Park Lane Hotel in 1943:

'The salmon does not feed in fresh water. No, but he does chew gum. . . . Consider, for example, the astonishing length of time that a salmon will keep a fly in his mouth before making up his mind that it is not very juicy and that it has no taste. People who have fished for salmon with big red worms will tell you that if a salmon has taken their worms into his mouth and has let go of them without being hooked, they find those worms of theirs no longer red, but pale, anaemic, empty, all their virtue gone. . . . Salmon in fresh water might not need to eat, but they were, like the Americans in that hotel, confirmed chewers. I have never chewed gum myself, but there were plenty of experts all round me who were ready to tell me what I wanted to know. . . . Different gums have different flavours and some are pleasanter than others. Obviously the thing to do was to devise a fly that should neither frighten nor irritate the salmon but should suggest to him that, *used as chewing gum*, it would enable him to recapture a flavour that he could remember enjoying.'

This led Ransome to consider which food organism the

A salmon leaping the Orrin Falls

salmon was most likely to have enjoyed recently, and he decided that it was the elver. It was not long before he had produced a fly, tied with feathers from a vulturine guineafowl, which exactly resembled an elver. This elver-fly is now a resounding success with salmon anglers, mainly on the west coast of Scotland, where the elvers enter the rivers in their thousands in the early summer.

One characteristic for which the salmon is famed is that of jumping. Even its specific name, *salar*, comes from the word *salire*, meaning to jump, and the Romans called the salmon 'Salar the leaper'. How it jumps waterfalls and what governs its chances of successful negotiation of these barriers were unknown until the late Dr T. A. Stuart of the Freshwater Fisheries Laboratory at Pitlochry solved the mystery by constant field observation and thorough laboratory experimentation. It turned out to be a matter of the relative depth of the water at the foot of the fall and the position of what is referred to in engineering terms as the 'standing wave', or hydraulic jump. This is a wave produced at the point of impact of the falling water on to the water below. If the standing wave is immediately below the fall, as it is in a vertical fall, and the depth of the water is one and a quarter times that of the height of the fall, then the lift produced by the standing wave, together with the inertia the salmon can achieve in that depth of water, is sufficient to enable it to clear the fall. The farther away the standing wave is from the point at which the descending water starts to fall, as on a sloping weir, the more difficult it is for the salmon to make a successful jump. The highest jump in Scotland was a vertical one of 12 ft at the Orrin Falls in Ross-shire (see page 16) but the height of this has been reduced by the installation of a wall a little farther downstream to ease ascent of the fall at the existing water levels which are dictated by the compensation flow arrangements at Orrin Dam some distance upstream.

There are a number of falls in Scotland where salmon may be seen jumping from the end of June onwards, and those which probably afford the best views are the Rogie Falls on the River Blackwater, near Strathpeffer in Ross-shire; the Falls of Shin, near Bonar Bridge in Sutherland; the Falls of Feugh, near Banchory on Royal Deeside; the Loups of the Burn on the North Esk, near Edzell in Angus; and the Pot of Gartness on the River Endrick near Loch Lomond.

After the salmon has been in fresh water for a few weeks it loses its silver coloration. A male, or 'cock fish', assumes a red and mottled appearance which is sometimes referred to as 'spawning tartan', and the fish itself as a 'soldier' or 'kipper'; the latter name is given to it probably because it is of value only if it has been smoked or 'kippered'. It also develops a thick spongy skin, an enlarged head and a well-developed hooked lower jaw known as a 'kype'. Such a drastic change in shape involves the redistribution of calcium which the salmon absorbs from its scales and deposits in its skull. The changes in the female, or 'hen fish', are not so dramatic. She becomes dark purple, and grey underneath. Her large orange eggs form much of her total body weight which, in making her so gravid, prevent her from negotiating severe obstacles close to spawning time.

A number of factors affect the movement of salmon up the river. In the spring, water temperature is of great importance, and until the temperature reaches 42 °F. (5 °C.) there is little upstream movement of fish over obstacles. Later in the season movement is affected by river flow and climatic conditions. Although there is no doubt that floods encourage salmon to move quickly upstream, the absence of spates does not prevent fish from ascending, and even during low-flow conditions salmon will swim upstream, provided it is possible for them to overcome any obstacles in their path. As the salmon start to mature near spawning time thyroid activity increases and there is an increase in the urgency of upstream movement.

I remember this 'sense of urgency' in the fish when I was supervising a salmon-research scheme on the Conon River system in Ross-shire. We had a number of trap sites, one of which was built below the Conon Falls. One section of this trap caught all the smolts descending the river, so that they could be counted, and the other section all ascending adults. After we had marked all the adults for individual identification should they return later, we released them downstream. During July and August few of the fish re-entered immediately, but by September, and from then until well into October, close to spawning time, the persistence of upstream movement increased. More fish released downstream after capture returned to the trap again almost immediately, and some came back as many as eight times.

As autumn approaches, the smaller streams with their clean beds of silt-free gravel and cool, well-oxygenated water are gradually occupied by the ripening adult. By early November spawning starts and, with the appearance of latecomers, may continue until well into January. There is a special ritual in spawning behaviour; this has been well documented by Dr J. W. Jones of Liverpool University in his New Naturalist monograph, *The Salmon* (1959). The ritual consists of the hen testing the gravel for its suitability, followed by exploratory digging, or 'cutting', of the gravel, after which a well-defined area is cut out to form a saucer-shaped depression. Cutting is carried out by the female turning on her side and producing a vigorous vertical flapping of her tail by alternately bending and straightening her body, dislodging the gravel which is carried downstream by the current. As the saucer-shaped depression gets deeper a mound of gravel appears on the downstream edge. When the nest, or 'redd' as the depression is called, is to the hen's liking she 'crouches' in the gravel in preparation for shedding the eggs. The cock fish, always in attendance, darts forward. Then, as the female opens her mouth wide, bends her body and ejects the eggs, the male starts to shed his milt. The covering of the eggs with gravel is carried out by the female moving upstream and dislodging the gravel in the manner described above.

The only signs that remain of spawning having taken place are mounds of freshly moved gravel lighter in colour than that of the surrounding stream bed, and saucer-shaped depressions of similarly clean gravel. The occasional fungus-covered salmon carcass lying in the slack water at the stream's edge bears witness to the stress incurred in the upstream fight to the spawning grounds and the last determined efforts to ensure the existence of future generations.

It is not surprising to find that virtually no male salmon, and only a small proportion of females, survive to return to spawn a second time. According to one authority the fish suddenly develop Cushing's disease caused by an increased output of the hormone A.C.T.H. (Adreno-Cortico-Tropic hormone). Apparently the salmon contains some internal 'clockwork' mechanism which turns up its pituitary controls at the time of migration, and the over-stimulated pituitary gland causes an excessive output of A.C.T.H. Another explanation for the high mortality is a severe reduction in body weight. Physiologists have found that death occurs in animals during starvation when the body weight is reduced by approximately 40 per cent. The loss of between 31 to 44 per cent in weight, according to the length of stay in the rivers, brings the salmon close to the limit of weight-loss endurance. As a result it is too weak on its return to the ocean to undergo normal recuperation. Salmon that spawn for a second time are recruited from the more vigorous individuals which manage to recover their strength before being subjected to a hostile environment.

All fish that have just finished spawning are referred to as 'kelts' until such time as they reach the sea. Some kelts return to the sea shortly after spawning, while others will not leave the river until March, April or even May. The kelt is an interesting creature, but unfortunately it gets short shrift from anglers fishing in the spring who unceremoniously haul it ashore, after a half-hearted struggle on the kelt's part, and, after releasing the treble hooks of their artificial minnow from the fish's bleeding jaws, return it to the water in disgust.

In recent years kelts have been less numerous and some

anglers maintain that the dearth of kelts in the lower reaches of rivers early in the year has resulted in the fresh spring fish passing on upstream more quickly; for it is said that newly returned salmon will join up with a shoal of kelts. William Scrope, the nineteenth-century writer on angling and stalking in Scotland, was emphatic about this habit: 'On the first arrival of the spring salmon from the sea, they are apt to take up their seats in the rear of a scull of kelts.'

During the remainder of the kelt's time in fresh water it gradually prepares for a renewed marine existence. Its scales soon resume their previous silver coloration, and just prior to its leaving fresh water a well-mended kelt can easily be mistaken for a clean salmon. Some people believe that kelts do feed in fresh water and blame them for taking the first young smolts on their journey to the sea. A concise report written as long ago as 1902 by Kingston Barton in the *Journal of Anatomy and Physiology* on 'The Digestive Tract in Kelts' leaves us in no doubt that the kelt stomach is active, and in the ones examined by him there was evidence of feeding having taken place.

Because of the low water temperatures in the early part of the year kelts are rather lethargic animals. In order to hasten the descent of a batch of kelts which had been previously stripped of their eggs at Loch Poulary on the Inverness-shire Garry to supply the Invergarry Hatchery, the late John Wood, Superintendent to the Ness District Salmon Fishery Board, and I carried out a kelt-transportation experiment. A small, numbered, tubular tag was attached to the base of the dorsal fin of each kelt which was then placed in a tank of aerated water on a lorry. The fish were taken all the way to the mouth of the River Ness where they were released. This would have been a long journey for the kelts if they had travelled by their normal route and would have involved negotiating Loch Garry, Loch Oich and Loch Ness. About 200 kelts were transported, and when Christmas arrived we felt that a satisfactory job had been completed and we could await the return of tags from anglers catching these fish when they came back to spawn a second time. Imagine our surprise at the start of the fishing season in January, when anglers sent in tags taken from our kelts—which were still kelts— caught in the River Ness, Loch Ness, Loch Oich and even as far upstream as Garry Dam. One can only assume that, as the fish had been stripped of their eggs artificially, they had wanted 'to do their own thing' and so had returned upstream.

So the kelts go back to the sea, some to return to spawn a second time, and being larger than many of the maiden fish, to make a particularly useful contribution of eggs.

Throughout the long winter months the large, orange, yolk-filled eggs lie under six or more inches of gravel and are swept by cool, well-oxygenated water. The eggs become 'eyed' by early January as the salmon embryos develop, the rate of development depending on water temperature. By the end of March the young salmon break out of the egg and at first bear little resemblance to a fish owing to the large yolk sac suspended from their 'stomach'. These young fish, or 'alevins', gradually absorb the yolk during the following four or five weeks as they make their way up through the gravel to the stream environment above. By the time they arrive their yolk sacs have virtually disappeared and they are miniature fish—'fry'—and are ready to feed. The term 'fry' is given to salmon during their first year of life, at the end of which time they are called 'parr'.

A little over a century ago the parr was thought to be a separate species, *Salmo salmulus*, and was considered so by a number of eminent naturalists including Turton, Willoughby, Yarrell, Sir Humphrey Davy and Sir William Jardine. However, Scrope, in his *Days and Nights of Salmon Fishing in the Tweed* (1843) was of a different, and correct, opinion when he said:

> 'Up to a late period it was universally thought that the spawn deposited as above mentioned was matured in a brief time, and that the young fry of the winter grew to six or seven inches long, were silver in colour, and went down

22

to the sea in this state with the first floods early in May of the coming spring. They were then called *smolts*. In the summer months there are always multitudes of little fry in every salmon river, which in the Tweed are called Parrs, and have been thought to be a different species from the Salmon. I have formerly held several tiresome arguments, both with practical men and also with naturalists, with an intent to convince them that they were one and the same species.

'The late Mr James Hogg, the Ettrick Shepherd, was particularly stiff and bristly in opinion against me. But he recanted afterwards and caused to be published in the famed "Maga" [*Blackwood's Magazine*] some account of experiments made by himself, all tending to confirm my theory.'

In fact in the 1830s John Shaw and Andrew Young had carried out salmon-breeding experiments at Stormontfield Ponds near Scone Palace on the banks of the Tay and had concluded that parr were the young of the salmon. The results of the experiments were summarised in *Blackwood's Magazine* (April 1840 and May 1843). However, the dispute raged on, and was documented in 1871 by Henry Flowerdew in a most interesting volume entitled *The Parr and Salmon Controversy*. It was re-issued in 1883 under the title *The Parr, Salmon Whitling and Yellow Fin Controversy*, in an expanded version to include a further debate involving the young of brown trout and sea trout.

On reaching a length of some three inches the salmon parr is very like a brown trout but displays conspicuous dark-blue thumb-marks (parr marks) along each side and has fewer spots than a trout; those which do occur tend to be above the central, or lateral, line. Other distinguishing features include the lack of the orange-red coloration on the tip of its small adipose fin situated on its back close to the tail. However, the most reliable and scientific way of distinguishing a salmon parr from a trout is by looking at its upper jaw. If the jaw bone, or maxilla, does not extend beyond an imaginary line dropped perpendicularly from the posterior edge of the iris of the eye, then the fish is a parr.

In any animal's life-history, a stage is reached where numbers are reduced, thereby controlling the population. With salmon, a high mortality rate occurs at the fry stage. Each fry, on starting to feed, establishes a territory on the stream bed, and it defends this from intruders by threat display. Those young fry which are unable to establish a territory have to disperse downstream and search elsewhere, and if unsuccessful they die from starvation or predation. As the fry grows and becomes a parr it requires a larger territory, and so by the end of the first year the initial fry population may have been reduced by as much as 90 to 95 per cent.

An interesting feature in the life of the parr is the precocious sexual maturation of a number of male parr in the autumn. The testes of the males become fully developed and the milt from them is capable of fertilising the eggs shed from an adult female. This process is referred to as 'paedogenesis' (Gr., creation by children) and well describes Nature's safety mechanism insuring the fertilisation of the eggs in the absence or shortage of adult males on the spawning grounds. It was this early maturation of some of the male parr which understandably led the early naturalists to believe that the parr was a separate species.

The age at which a parr goes to sea as a smolt depends on how long it takes it to grow to a length of four or five inches; as has been shown, when a parr reaches this length it usually becomes a smolt in the coming spring. So if it reached a length of, say, four inches in August, then one could safely expect it to become a smolt in the following spring.

The transformation of the parr to the smolt stage starts in late March when, with increasing thyroid activity, a subcutaneous silvery deposit of guanin—a constituent of nucleic acids—is laid down which conceals the parr markings and turns the fish silver. In the final stages of its change the tail fin becomes black and the fish is a true smolt.

There are many factors which trigger off the downstream movement of smolts and these include rise in water temperature and increased river flow as a result of rain. During the early part of the smolt migration, movement is during the hours of darkness, but by late May and early June movement occurs during the middle part of the day. Of the fry that emerge from the gravel only about 3 to 5 per cent reach the smolt stage; of these rarely more than 10 per cent survive to become smolts, and usually nearer 6 per cent will return to the river as adult salmon.

It seems likely that smolts need some time to become acclimatised to saline conditions and it has been noticed that before entering the sea they often remain in the estuary for a short time, probably for this purpose.

Once the smolt enters the sea little is known of its subsequent movements. However, with the advent of the Greenland fishery and the high-seas fisheries off Iceland, the Faroes and Spitzbergen, much more has come to be known about the sea life of salmon. Between 1884 and 1954 there were fewer than eighty Scottish records of salmon taken at sea, and these described the capture of approximately 90 'clean' salmon, 10 salmon kelts, 5 grilse and 3 pre-grilse. Much of the early information was collected from examinations of the stomachs of other fish. This is particularly useful as it gives us an idea of the sources of mortality at sea. Among the fish recorded eating salmon are the cod, halibut, ling, lythe or pollack, porbeagle shark and skate.

The sea food of salmon consists chiefly of fish such as capelin, herring, sand eels and sprats, and the larger animals found in plankton. A Danish scientist estimated that more than sixteen tons of sprats are eaten by the exploitable part of the Baltic salmon stock in a year, and he also considered that the growth-rate of adult salmon is largely determined by the amount of food available during the first few months in the sea.

Although it is now known, perhaps regrettably, where some of the salmon's sea-feeding areas are, the means by which they return to their parent rivers still remain a mystery. While we as terrestrial beings can appreciate how birds and mammals migrate it is difficult for us to determine the migratory mechanisms used by aquatic animals. Perhaps it is a combination of ocean currents and navigation by the stars, the moon and the sun, for salmon, being pelagic, live in the surface waters and so may be able to detect changes in the heavens. Once the fish approach the coast new stimuli probably take over, although current-systems may well play an important role until the fish are within the influence of their parent river systems.

An interesting theory put forward by Dr Leslie Stewart in a talk to the Atlantic Salmon Association in Canada in 1977, and printed in the *Salmon and Trout Magazine* for July 1978, is one referred to as the gyre theory. A gyre is a rotating current in the ocean, and Dr Stewart suggests that when a smolt leaves the coastal waters it will come within the influence of an oceanic gyre, or current, in which it will drift along. During this time it will feed on marine organisms, the degree of feeding increasing or decreasing according to the physiological condition of the fish. At certain times it may leave and rejoin or even transfer to other associated gyres. The ultimate result, if it kept within its original gyre, would be its return to the point at which it embarked as a smolt. The lack of oceanic gyres owing to the absence of integral land masses is the explanation Dr Stewart gives for the failure of Atlantic salmon to establish sea-going populations when introduced into the southern hemisphere.

Another theory is based on odour perception, and two North American scientists, Hasler and Wisby, demonstrated the importance of stream odours in the orientation of Pacific salmon. This was first considered by Frank Buckland in 1880 when he suggested that salmon were assisted by their power of smell to find their way in the sea, as well as to find their parent river. Others believe that salmon return to their breeding grounds by a wandering mechanism rather than a homing one. However, in recent years evidence has been presented by Dr David Solomon in *Nature* (vol. 244, 28 July,

1973) which indicates that the homing of adult salmon may be largely dependent on the presence of other individuals in the river and that a metabolic product of a discrete population could be the odour to which adults home. Some time earlier another scientist, Dr H. Nordeng, put forward evidence to indicate that the homing of a migratory population of char in Norway was influenced by pheromones and suggested that the attractant might be secreted in the mucus. With the greatest respect, I feel that these last two theories have more scientific merit than that proposed by Eric Linklater, when he referred to the returning adult salmon which 'recognise, by taste or scent, the flavour or the odour of broth (minute particles of dead fish—fish meal or an oily effluent from the larger, more quickly decomposing carcases) brewed in their own river, and follow it out of the tide and into fresh water'. However, the following passage from *The Secret Larder* aptly brings this chapter to a close:

'Instinct, perhaps, is stimulated by an ancestral taint; and from the corruption of death there goes out perpetually the incentive to new procreations.'

Scotch Salmon

THE early Norse and Icelandic invaders must have been impressed by the wealth of salmon in our rivers, for they gave their name for salmon, *lax*, to quite a number of them. There is the River Laxford in north-west Sutherland, the River Laxay in east Lewis, the Laxdale River in west Harris and the Laxadale River and Laxadale Lochs in east Harris.

During the centuries after the visits of the Vikings, visitors to Scotland were continually astounded by the abundance of salmon. In 1498, the Spanish Ambassador, Don Pedro de Ayala, commented on the immense quantities of salmon that were taken out of the Beauly and the Spey, and 160 years later the Cromwellian trooper, Richard Franck, described the plentiful catches at the various fishing centres. On a visit to Stirling he remarked that 'the abundance of salmon hereabouts is hardly to be credited'; and at Inverness: 'Truly I stood amazed to see such companies of salmon.' A hundred years on, Captain Burt, writing from Inverness, said that the price of salmon was a penny a pound, and that 'the meanest servants who are not at board wages will not make a meal upon salmon if they can get anything else to eat'. Daniel Defoe, on his rambles through Scotland, remarked that 'the rivers Dee and Don afford salmon in the greatest plenty that can be imagined'. Another traveller of nearly the same period, describing himself as 'A Gentleman', began his book with: 'The salmon-fishery is particularly the delight and the boast of the Scotch, insomuch that for it they too much neglect all the rest.' Speaking of Perth, the same writer said: 'The salmon taken here, and all over the Tay, are extremely good, and the quantity prodigious. They convey them to Edinburgh, and to all the towns where they have no salmon, and barrel-up great quantities for exportation.' The 'Gentleman's' remarks on the Ness were supported by another author of the same period, Heron, who said in his

28

book *Scotland Delineated* that 'the salmon fishery which is very considerable, is let to London fishmongers'—an interesting development to be sure.

The wealth of Scottish rivers was nowhere more evident than in the Tweed. Sir William Brereton in his travels in 1636 referred to the river, at Berwick, being 'most infinitely stored with salmon, one hundred or two hundred salmons at one draught; but much more was reported by our host, which is almost incredible, that there were two thousand salmons taken since Sunday last' (the dates would have been 17th to 25th June). The naturalist Pennant, in his *Tour of Scotland and Voyage to the Hebrides* (1774), remarked of the Tweed at Berwick that a boatload of salmon, and sometimes nearly double that quantity, was often taken in a single tide; and according to the Reverend Richard Warner (1802) a total of 1·6 million pounds of salmon were dispatched from Berwick annually.

It is no wonder that Scotland has been a salmon-producing country for centuries, probably ever since she traded with other countries, and certainly since medieval times. Initially the salmon were salted or pickled before dispatch. In the thirteenth century, Aberdeen, Perth, Berwick and Glasgow were already centres of the salmon trade and many a family owed its wealth, at least in part, to this plentiful species. French, German and Italian merchants journeyed to Scotland to purchase fish, bringing in exchange cloth, velvet, silks, spices and wine. The shipment of salmon to Flanders and France began as early as 1380, and according to Thomazi in his *Histoire de la Pêche*, there was a Scottish decree of the fourteenth century stipulating that French merchants had to pay for their salmon partly with silver and partly with wine.

In a report of a tour by Thomas Tucker in 1655 (*Report by Thomas Tucker upon the Settlement of the Revenues of Excise and Customs in Scotland*) it was noted that lasts of salmon were being shipped out from Banff, Garmouth, Findhorn, Aberdeen and Montrose, and almost certainly from Leith and Dunbar, as was noted by Jorevin de Rocheford in 1661.

A last is a load, usually estimated at 4,000 lb., and as sixty lasts of salmon were sent out from Garmouth and Findhorn in a year it implied an export of some 240,000 lb. of salmon—no mean export in those days.

By the end of the eighteenth century a certain George Dempster revolutionised salmon marketing by shipping fish in ice from the River Tay to London, and by 1838 there was a regular transport service from Edinburgh to Billingsgate Market. The advent of the railway further speeded up the transportation of fish and expanded the demand for what surely must be one of the most nutritious, most palatable, as well as the most appealing sources of fat and protein.

Nowadays commercial catches of salmon from the sweep nets at the river mouth and the bag nets and stake nets along the coast are dispatched by rail and road from Aberdeen, Montrose, Perth, Glasgow and Berwick to London, Manchester, as well as to other cities and the Continent. In some instances salmon are flown to Continental and Scandinavian buyers. Salmon surplus to the immediate demands are blast-frozen and stored until required, and others are smoked for the luxury market. Fish caught by angling tenants are taken to the nearest railway station each evening by the head ghillie and sent south in their straw matts. Salmon fetch a very high price on the market nowadays; a spring salmon costs somewhere in the region of £3·50 per lb. and smoked salmon £4·50 per lb. However, the rates and rents for salmon fishing on the better waters are extremely high and most owners and tenants of fishings find that they have to sell the majority of their fish to meet these expenses which, for owners of fishings particularly, can be crippling.

Gone are the days when salmon was a staple food in the diet of many country folk. According to Richard Kerr in his *General View of the County of Berwick* (1809) all farmhouses in the Vale of Tweed depended upon salmon for a considerable portion of their winter food supply. This conflicts to some extent with the observations of the Revd. James Hall in his *Travels in Scotland by an Unusual Route* (1805), who remarked that 'this species of food is generally too dear to be used by the common people . . .'. Of course it depends on how the farmers in 'Tweed Vale' came by their salmon, as leistering (spearing) for salmon was a favourite pastime— one vividly described by Scott in *Guy Mannering*, as well as by Scrope and Stoddart.

In those times, although there was often a glut of salmon at Berwick and Perth, there might be a dearth in London, and probably a complete absence in Nottingham and Derby. An amusing story was told by Captain Burt in 1730 of a Highland laird going to a London hotel with his ghillie, and, from motives of frugality, ordering a beef-steak for himself and 'salmon for the laddie'. On reckoning with his host, he discovered he had to pay a shilling for his own dinner and a guinea for the laddie's!

Many stories have been told about the clause in the indentures of apprentices which is supposed to have stated that salmon was not to be served to them at more than two meals a week; this was sometimes increased to three or even four meals. According to I. Cohen in 'Apprentices and Salmon', a paper in the *Transactions of the Woolhope Naturalists' Field Club, Hertfordshire* (Vol. XXXV, Part 1, 1955), the earliest reference appeared in 1658 and is referred to in Richard Franck's *Northern Memoirs*. However, search has proved that no Act, Statute or Ordinance regarding the serving of salmon to apprentices is recorded. Mr Cohen also mentions a correspondence in *The Scotsman* in 1946, which was sparked off by a statement about the salmon legend in G. N. Trevelyan's *Social History*. Although some of the correspondence referred to farm workers insisting on a diet of salmon being limited to a certain number of days in the week, there was no mention of the eating habits of apprentices. An exhaustive search of several thousand indentures and records from the fourteenth century to the present day led Mr Cohen to conclude that 'there never was such a clause'. There is no fear of today's apprentices being overwhelmed by a surfeit of salmon.

However, the Scottish salmon fishery remains a very viable industry. In 1975, for example, the catch of salmon and grilse, by nets and rods, was 209,738 and 214,251, respectively. The estimated value of the total salmon catch by all methods for that year was £3,337,730, and 1,247 men were directly employed in salmon net-fishing. The indirect value of rod-caught fish is more difficult to assess because there are spin-offs for so many—ghillies, hotel owners, shopkeepers, fishing-tackle manufacturers, and so on.

With the upsurge in angling and tourism there have been great changes in salmon fishing. Many more beats on famous rivers are now available to the public through angling associations and angling-instruction holidays run by hotels, and owners of salmon fishings are having to let their beats for part of the year to cover the overheads incurred in running estates. Americans, Germans, Dutch, Belgians and Swiss are often the only ones who can afford the high charges demanded, although sometimes syndicates of Scottish or English anglers rent beats from one year to the next by clubbing together. When rivers or estates come on to the market, the purchasers are normally people from the Continent, or some large investment trust or insurance company.

Finally, mention should be made of the ownership of salmon fisheries. In Scotland they are a separate heritable estate. This means that the title, or right of ownership, does not go automatically with ownership of the land adjoining the fisheries. Therefore it is quite common for one party to own the land on the banks of a river and another to own the right of salmon fishing in it. This situation grew out of the legal position of the salmon fisheries in the feudal era when most of the titles were first granted. Originally all land in Scotland, as well as the salmon fisheries, was the property of the Crown. When land was granted by charter to persons other than the Crown, the grant, because of the great value of the salmon fisheries, did not carry the fisheries with it, unless the charter specifically said so. Thus, long after most of the land had been granted by charter to subjects, the Crown retained ownership of many of the salmon fisheries. About

30 per cent of coastal salmon fishing remains Crown property and is administered by the Crown Estate Commissioners.

Only a limited amount of fresh water is now so held; from an early period many salmon-fishing rights were conveyed to individuals by means of written Crown grants. All private titles to salmon fishing are derived from such grants and must be based on deeds recorded in the Register of Sasines, kept at Meadowbank House in Edinburgh. Orkney and Shetland are exceptions in that much of the land is held under Udal or Norse law, whereby salmon fisheries are a pertinent of the land, as are ordinary freshwater fisheries elsewhere in Scotland.

A unique right of access to salmon fishing is invested in the Kindly Tenants—the tenants of the Royal Four Towns of Hightae, Greenhill, Heck and Smallholm. They were granted the salmon fishing rights over four miles of the Annan by King Robert the Bruce. Those who are on the electoral role have the right to fish for salmon free of charge. This was made statutory under a recent Act of Parliament. Tenants who pay rent to the landlord, the Earl of Mansfield, are also entitled to this privilege.

Catching Salmon:
Methods Ancient and Modern

MANY of the early methods used for catching salmon were aboriginal in their simplicity and included spears of various types, large barbed hooks tied on to lengths of wood and referred to as cleeks or gaffs, baskets and hand nets. In some situations they were extremely effective and served the local people well enough to ensure that salmon were part of their staple diet at certain times of the year. Although these methods are now outlawed, they are worth describing because they were so much part of the Scottish rural scene.

The salmon spear, the leister or waster (see page 36), was in use at least as early as the sixteenth century. The term 'leister' was first mentioned in the Charters of the Royal Burgh of Ayr, 1593, and the term 'waster' was recorded in the Register of the Great Seal of Scotland in 1580. The spear consists of a wooden shaft attached by a socket to an arrangement of iron prongs which vary in number from one to seven. The prongs may be single or double barbed. Leistering was commonly done at night, with the aid of a torch called a 'blaze' to attract the fish; the expression 'burning the water' referred to the act of leistering. According to the Register of the Privy Council in 1601, leistering appears to have been forbidden, but it was an accepted way of catching fish on the Tweed until the Tweed Fisheries Act of 1857, and it even had a close season from 15th October to 14th February. The reason the leister was used legally on Border rivers long after it was banned elsewhere in Scotland was no doubt due to the encouragement leistering received from Acts of the Scottish Parliament in force before the Union. In an exception to the general Salmon Act passed in the Ninth Parliament of James I in 1429, it is declared 'that the waters of Solway and Tweede sall be reddie to all Scottishmen all times of the zeir, als lang as Berwick and Roxburgh are in the Englishmannis hands'.

With the 1857 Act, however, the leister was banned and the Tweed Amendment Act of 1859 made it an offence to be in possession of a leister within five miles of the river. Prior to that time leistering was often a social event, and one in which Sir Walter Scott was known to participate. According to Tom Stoddart, the nineteenth-century Border angler and author, 'as many fish were sometimes killed by this method in a single night as would suffice to exercise the ingenuity and encourage the perseverence of twenty honest anglers throughout the season'. Stoddart wrote a stirring poem called 'The Leisterers' Song' which conjures up the excitement of such an escapade:

'Glances the shining spear
From harmless hands unheeded!
On, in its swift career,
The dream-like fish hath speeded.

It is the leisterer's cry!
The salmon, ho! oho!
Along its wake the torches break,
And waver to and fro.

Wildly the eager band
Closes its fatal numbers;
Across its glistening sand
The wizard water slumbers.

It is the leisterer's cry!
The salmon, ho! oho!
And, lightning like, the white prongs strike
The jaded fish below.

Rises the cheering shout,
Over the rapid slaughter;
The gleaming torches float
The old, oak-shadowed water.

It is the leisterer's cry!
The salmon, ho! oho!
Calmly it lies, and gasps and dies,
Upon the mossy bank low!'

Salmon leistering. From a painting by Tom Scott (National Galleries of Scotland)

It was the illegal use of the leister during spawning time which probably decided the Tweed Commissioners to ban it, and perhaps the efforts of John Younger of St Boswells played some little part in making them reach their decision when the following passage appeared in 1847 in one of his articles:

'Then the fish run up in shoals to spawn, under protection of the upper water proprietors, to whom, properly speaking, close-time is of no special benefit. Such a dialogue as this may at times be heard between a farmer's servant and his master at close-time—"Maister, twa or three o' us are thainking o' lighting a bit bleeze at the *reds* the night, up at the Shaw-brae-fords, whar we saw them tum'lin up this afternoon, like brewer's swine drunk on maut-draff."

' "Weel, Davie, I daresay, for my part at least, ye may just take what ye can get when ye have them here, as I am sure I havna seen three good fish in our water through a' the simmer. They *kep* them a' about *Berwick* an' *Norham* now, wi' their lang nets, except jist a while at the tail o' the season, when the floodings get ower heavy for their net works." So, under such supreme permission, Davie raises a band perhaps nearly as strong as Rob Roy's black-mail clan, and such as a regiment of dragoons could scarcely capture, kill, or disperse.

'Thus the havoc proceeds, indiscriminately, on fish in all respect out of season; and half-spawned or newly-spawned salmon is certainly most disgusting food; though, as a poacher would say, "a fish is a fish, if you can catch it, when, where, and how you can". And this is pursued recklessly, regardless of the depreciation of the value of the fish, or the destructive effects on the species to future generations.'

Although the leister is now a museum piece, the cleek is still used, and many salmon and sea trout are hooked off the redds on Tweedside each autumn. With the first rise of the water in late October and November, spawning fish move out of the upper Tweed and into the streams around Peebles. With them come at darkening the unscrupulous who, with the aid of lights, rake and tear at the spawn-laden fish in the hope of making a 'quick buck' by the clandestine sale of the carcasses for smoking.

There is no sport in the capture of fish by this means, and such folk can have little pride in their nefarious activities. It was entirely different for the horseman on the Solway who used lances to capture their fish, and none other than Sir Walter Scott's Redgauntlet displayed his skill at the sport:

'The scene was animated by the exertions of a number of horsemen, who were actually employed in hunting salmon. Ay, Alan, lift up your hands and eyes as you will, I can give their mode of fishing no name so appropriate; for they chased the fish at full gallop, and struck them with their barbed spears, as you see hunters spearing boars in the old tapestry. The salmon, to be sure, take the thing more quietly than the boars; but they are so swift in their own element, that to pursue and strike them is the task of a good horseman, with a quick eye, a determined hand, and full command both of his horse and weapon. The shouts of the fellows as they galloped up and down in the animating exercise—their loud bursts of laughter when any of their number caught a fall—and still louder acclamations when any of the party made a capital stroke with his lance—gave so much animation to the whole scene.'

An old method of catching salmon—and one used long ago by the North American Indians—was by means of a basket. At the Falls of Tummel and other falls, a wide-mouthed basket was hung by a chain from a rock close to where salmon regularly jumped. The fish unsuccessful in their endeavours as often as not fell back into the basket. At the fall of Arkaig, near Achnacarry House, matters were so arranged that the salmon not only fell into the basket, but in so doing rang a bell in the kitchen to announce its arrival, and, as it were, to advise the cook to put the water on to boil.

Various types of hand nets were used in Scotland in the past; these included Herry-water nets, triangle nets, stoop nets, ladle nets and shoulder nets. The only hand net still in use is the haaf net, which is employed in the tidal waters of the Solway Firth. Haaf nets are mounted on a wooden frame, about 16 ft by 4 ft, with a handle attached to the middle of one of the long sides. The fisherman stands in the tide with the middle stick over his shoulder and the net streaming behind him. When he feels a fish strike he lifts the lower lip to prevent the fish from escaping. The fisherman must place himself within a few yards of the probable course of moving fish. It is customary for a number of men to fish together. They stand side by side facing the current of the tide and as the tide rises the outermost man in turn transfers himself to the inner end. The procedure is repeated in the reverse order as the tide recedes.

A type of net unique to the Galloway Dee and still in use is the yair net. A yair consists of two converging fences, or leaders, made of stakes interwoven with saplings to form a coarse wicker work. In the apex of the 'V' formed by the converging leaders is a rectangular opening, and across the top of it is a platform with a box on which the fisherman sits. The actual net is a deep bag. The fisherman lowers it into the opening so that the water flows through it, and sits holding a system of lines leading from the open end of the bag. If a fish touches the end of the bag, he feels the impact through the lines, and immediately hauls up the mouth of the net, thus securing it.

Two other nets used in the Solway district are the whammel net and the poke net. The whammel is a type of drift net used only to a limited extent, but from a decision made by a Scottish court in 1962 it appears that the use of whammel nets on the Scottish side of the main channel of the Solway Firth is now illegal. However, the poke net is used exclusively on the Scottish side of the Solway Firth. Poke nets are

Various methods of catching salmon, the River Moriston, Inverness-shire. Illustrations from Cordiner's Views, or Remarkable Ruins and Romantic Prospects, by the Rev Charles Cordiner of Banff (1788)

mounted in lines on rows of poles and consist of a series of pockets of net in which fish are enmeshed.

Many methods used for trapping salmon come under the all-embracing term 'fixed engines'. A fixed engine means any engine—that is, contrivance—net or trap used for the taking of salmon, other than a sweep net which when in use is hauled through the water continuously and is not allowed to become stationary in the water or to drift with the current.

In Scotland the principal fixed engines in use today are the bag net (see page 42) and the stake net. The bag net is commonly used on rocky coasts and consists essentially of a trap made of netting to which fish are directed by a leader, that is, a line of netting placed across the route the salmon usually follow as they move along the coast. The salmon swim towards the leader but cannot get through and instinctively turn seawards. Swimming along the leader they are led into the mouth of the net and through a succession of compartments into a final chamber, or fish court.

Stake nets, known as flynets or 'jumpers' depending on their construction, are used on sandy shores and consist of walls of netting erected on stakes set into the sea bed, which act as leaders to approaching salmon. At intervals pockets or traps are inserted to take the fish that are directed along the leader. Unlike bag nets, they do not float but are fixed to the sea bed throughout their length.

Other fixed engines at one time used in the rivers, but which are now illegal, were cruives, doachs, stell nets and cairn nets. Cruives consisted of weirs, or cruive-dikes, in which were incorporated cruive-boxes, or traps. These are still present on some rivers, such as the Conon and the Beauly, but are no longer operational. Doachs were used on the Kirkcudbrightshire Dee and were rather like cruives. They consisted of a masonry wall joining various outcropping rocks and extending across the bed of the river from bank to bank. In the wall were three gaps which let the water through, but which could be closed to the larger fish by removable 'hecks'. These were wooden gratings with vertical

Fishing a salmon bag net. From a painting by John Chambers

bars a minimum of three inches apart. All fish too large to pass between the bars were held back and scooped out of the pools downstream with ladle nets which were outsize landing nets with 20-ft shafts.

The net and coble is the only method of net fishing which is legal inside estuary limits throughout Scotland. The net is loaded on to a coble, a small flat-bottomed boat, and attached to the net is a rope held by a fisherman on the shore. Once the operation begins, he must keep the rope in motion by his own exertions. The coble is propelled across the estuary or river, and the net is shot as it goes. The course is roughly a semicircle finishing on the shore from which the boat started out. The ends of the net are then hauled in and the fish removed. It is an essential part of net-and-coble fishing that the net is hauled through the water in one continuous movement by the fishermen, who in some areas have the assistance of power winches. The net must not be allowed to become stationary or drift with the tide, as the fish taken in the net are only guided to the landing area, not enmeshed in it. The central and deeper part of the net—the 'bosom'—is generally bag-shaped and the fishermen drive the fish towards it by splashing the ropes on the wings of the net as it is being pulled in.

A modified—and illegal—method of fishing with a net and coble, used on some parts of the west coast, is the toot and haul net. Instead of being drawn as soon as it is shot, the net is set across the stream, or out from the shore if it is done on the coast, the staff at one end of the net being fastened to a rope attached to a windlass. In this way the ropes attached to each end of the net are ashore and the net is held stretched out in position by the boat which anchors about twenty yards or so from the end of the net, and is turned back towards the shore so as to form a bend. The man in the boat remains on the look-out and in touch with the net. When he sees fish within the bounds of the net, he signals—toots—to the men on shore and sets the net free for them to haul it in at once.

Drift-net fishing has in recent years developed as a means of catching salmon off the Scottish coast, and also on the high

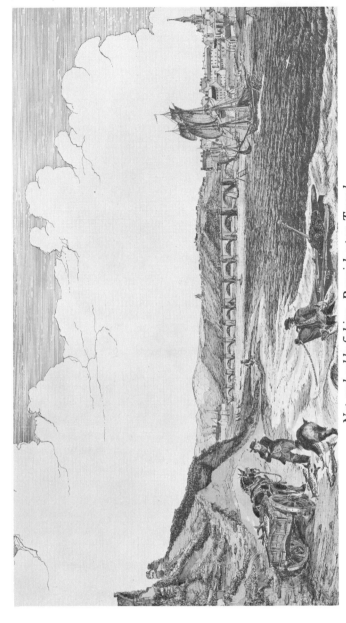

Net-and-coble fishing, Berwick-upon-Tweed
(Adapted from an unsigned engraving and redrawn by D. S. Halley)

seas. Because the monofilament used in the nets is virtually invisible in the water, it makes them very effective for enmeshing salmon. Although this method of fishing is now illegal it is still used extensively at sea, and also from the shore, particularly on the west coast and around the Outer Isles. This problem is discussed in the final chapter.

There is no doubt that the most exciting way of catching salmon is by angling, using rod, line and lure; countless books have been written on the subject. The main ways of luring salmon by rod and line are with artificial flies and fish, and with natural bait such as live earthworms, preserved fish, prawns and shrimps. The development of fishing tackle has increased rapidly in recent years. In the past salmon rods were long (up to 20 ft) and heavy, being built of greenheart or split cane; the cumbersome reels were made of brass. Our angling forefathers must have had stronger physiques and constitutions than we have today, for not only did they walk greater distances while fishing but frequently they waded in the water without waterproof boots. Scrope had a rule of thumb concerning wading which nowadays would send us to our beds with heavy colds at the very thought:

'Never go into the water deeper than the fifth button of your waistcoat [he does not say whether it is the fifth from the top or fifth from the bottom]; even this does not always agree with tender constitutions in frosty weather. As you are likely not to take a just estimate of the cold in the excitement of the sport, should you be of a delicate temperament, and be wading in the month of February when it may chance to freeze very hard, pull down your stockings and examine your legs. Should they be black, or even purple, it might be as well to get on dry land; but if they are only rubicund, you may continue to enjoy the water, if it so pleases you.'

Salmon rods have tended to become shorter, and with the introduction of synthetic materials fibreglass and carbon-

Brothers of the angle

fibre rods are replacing the more traditional split-cane rods. In reel manufacture brass has been replaced by light alloys and the development of the fixed-spool and multiplier spinning reels has produced efficient pieces of equipment which enable the novice angler to achieve a high standard of casting in a short time. Synthetic fibres such as nylon and Terylene have taken over from the more expensive plaited silk lines in some branches of angling. Development has also continued with flies and lures. Flies have become smaller and hair has to some extent replaced the more expensive and exotic feathers used in fly-dressing in the past. Artificial minnows are being replaced in the angler's tackle box by pieces of metal called 'spoons'. The trend has been towards less elaborate tackle and more efficient methods of fishing. In some ways this is sad, because a lot of the charm, tradition and skill is disappearing. Few are the salmon anglers nowadays who, with a steep bank behind them, can effortlessly Spey-cast a long line across a fast river. It is so much easier to throw out a heavy piece of metal from a reel that is guaranteed not to overrun. The salmon flies themselves are losing some of their grace. In yesteryear the angler's fly-box was graced with romance and humour, containing flies with such names as Lady Caroline and the Lady of Mertoun, Meg with the Muckle Mouth and Meg in her Braws. Other flies had equally entrancing names: Durham Ranger, Green Highlander, Jock Scott, Thunder and Lightning, and Hairy Mary. All were beautifully dressed with exotic feathers, and the destruction of one became a personal loss. Nowadays our powers of description are failing; flies appear with names like Black and Yellow, and old names are given to new dressings which bear no resemblance to the original. Some sceptics argue that it does not matter what colour the feathers of a salmon fly are, as the fish can distinguish only shades of black and white. This, of course, is not true. The retina of the salmon's eye contains cells similar to the colour-sensing rods and cones found in the retinas of other vertebrate animals. There is other evidence too that the salmon not only has good eyesight but can also distinguish colours.

With increasing affluence fishing is becoming accessible to everyone. However, on the whole salmon angling remains an expensive sport because of the high rents which are charged on the rivers; therefore sport fishing for salmon is a valuable national asset.

Struggle for Survival

> I am, Sir, a brother of the Angle, and therefore an enemy to
> the Otter; for you are to note that we Anglers all love one
> another, and therefore do I hate the Otter, both for my own
> and for their sakes who are of my brotherhood.

IZAAK Walton wrote these words in 1653 in *The Compleat
Angler*; but if he was angling today and wanted to express his
sentiments by taking violent action against the otter, he
would be liable to prosecution in England and Wales under
the Conservation of Wild Creatures and Wild Plants Act,
1975, which the otter joined on 1st January 1978. This shows
a welcome degree of enlightment among the sporting frater-
nity, a number of whom supported the proposed statutory
protection of the otter. At one time this sector of the com-
munity tended to encourage the slaughter of all birds and
mammals that competed with or preyed upon the quarry
they themselves were interested in hunting. Such natural
predators of the salmon as goosanders, red-breasted mer-
gansers, cormorants, shags (none of which is protected in
Scotland under the Protection of Birds Act, 1954), grey seals
and mink were, and to some extent still are, among those
killed for their habit of eating salmon. Although the named
birds undoubtedly eat young salmon, their low numerical
density on any one river precludes them from being a serious
threat to salmon stocks in Scotland. The mink's fish diet
consists chiefly of eels, but it does take trout and young
salmon. However, it is probably as unwelcome with the
poultry breeder and ornithologist as it is with the fisherman.

The grey seal is more of a problem. It is a large animal and
eats in the region of 150 pounds of fish a day. It is common
around the coast of Scotland, and as it frequents inshore
waters it is inevitable that at certain times of the year salmon
forms a large part of its diet. Various estimates have been

49

made of the number of salmon taken by grey seals; one of these indicates that over a five-year period 150,000 salmon and sea trout were killed by seals on the Scottish east coast. In addition to the fish killed, there are those that are badly mutilated and which, if caught later by fishermen, can be sold only as 'seconds', fetching a low price on the market. Commercial fishermen are also bothered by the damage seals inflict on their nets, and so it is no wonder that the Department of Agriculture and Fisheries and the Nature Conservancy Council are pressurised to allow some control of seal numbers. Culling of young seals is carried out each autumn, but frequently the weather is so bad that the desired level of cull is not achieved.

Predation is a natural phenomenon and is only a problem when man wants a larger proportion of the available harvest. There is, of course, the antisocial person who feels entitled to a share to which he has no legal right, although he may argue that he has a 'natural right'—he is the poacher. Few would condemn the character—such as Shiner in Henry Williamson's *Salar the Salmon*—who wants 'one for the pot' and who is as much a part of the wild as the wild things themselves. Far worse are the gangs of toughs from the cities who come out to the rivers, when the fish are congregating below the falls, and tip in a tinful of cyanide and kill not two or three but scores of fish, frequently more than they can carry away. In one incident alone in 1977 over one hundred salmon were killed in this way on a famous salmon river in Angus. The number of young fish killed in these poisoning incidents is never known, as gulls soon remove the evidence.

Gang-poaching is not a recent innovation and is probably not even carried out with the same ruthlessness as it was in days of yore. John Younger gives a vivid account of a poaching scene on the spawning redds:

'But of all fresh water piracies, desperate, daring, cruel and devilish, is the leistering or spearing with night lights, and being prevented from all other more sportsman-like methods, this the poachers fall upon, and will effect their purpose by, in spite of all the police force that can conveniently be arrayed against them. Leistering can be effected on spawn beds, by two or three individuals, one to hold the torch, another to use the spear. But as, in the use of lights, they have no sufficient protection from a surprise from the bailiffs, the poachers associate in bands of twenties, thirties or fifties (poor fellows, at that season idle, and therefore daring and desperate) from all the districts around, and, disguised in rags and blackened faces, proceed, like tribes of Indians, to the massacre. Rushing to the spawning gravel beds, over which the flaming lights are kindled, behold fifty or a hundred pairs of fish all promiscuously slaughtered in the very act of spawning, and (as I presume) of impregnation for the succeeding season.

'A dozen of bailiffs, who have stolen to the spot with a view to prevention, look stupefied while standing on a cliff of a winter night, in witness of such a scene as this, more bewildered than was "Tam o'Shanter" when viewing the witches' dance to the devil's piping.'

One fish which is particularly fond of young salmon is the pike, a voracious creature which can grow to a very large size; specimens exceeding 30 lb. have been taken from a number of Scottish lochs. From an examination of the stomachs of 3,000 pike taken from the Conon River system in Ross-shire I estimated that the pike population in one tributary, the River Bran, had one year eaten 10 per cent of the smolts going to sea. There are problems connected with the control of pike owing to the fact that they are truly cannibals. It is not uncommon on opening the stomach of a large pike to find another pike inside and yet another inside the stomach of the swallowed one—rather like a set of Russian dolls. When one tries to control pike by netting, the first result is that the largest are removed and, with the consequent decrease in average size, there is less cannibalism. However, the remaining fish eat young salmon but not large brown trout, which also find young salmon appetising. So there is an intermediate period when more young salmon are eaten, until netting reaches the stage where the numbers of pike are drastically reduced.

Disease is a scourge which can be far more serious than predation; outbreaks of bacterial and viral infections have a drastic effect on the adult salmon population in particular. A common bacterial disease is furunculosis. This is most noticeable during the warmer months when river levels are low and salmon are concentrated in pools waiting for more water to allow them to continue their upstream journey. The symptoms consist of boils, or furuncles; they disfigure the fish and it soon dies. One form of the disease is so acute that it can cause death within twenty-four hours of the fish entering the infected area.

Ulcerative dermal necrosis (U.D.N.) is one of the most serious diseases ever to affect salmon, and unfortunately the causative organism has never been isolated and identified. It is not a bacterial disease but is almost certainly caused by a virus. The first signs are the appearance of small bleached areas on the head, back and tail. As the disease progresses, areas of bluish-grey slimy growth develop on the bleached areas, making the fish very conspicuous in the water. Later, more patches appear and the existing ones spread over large areas of the head, back and the wrist of the tail. These may become ulcerated and then infected with fungus.

It is almost certain that U.D.N. is the disease which affected Scottish salmon in the 1880s, decimating stocks. In the present century outbreaks of the disease first appeared in some rivers in 1966 and gradually spread through Scotland in the succeeding years, although it has not occurred in some of the rivers in the north-west and in the Outer Isles. It is difficult to estimate how many salmon have fallen victim to the disease since it first appeared, but between March 1967 and 25th February 1968, a total of 41,234 infected salmon and grilse were removed from Scottish rivers. The disease is still present in some rivers, notably the Tweed, the Doon, the Awe and the Aberdeenshire Dee, but there is some sign that the fish, through several generations, are developing an immunity to it.

The salmon, like most animals, is a home for parasites, but rarely are these harmful, and in fact there is one, the sea louse, that is welcomed by the angler. It is a little brown organism, 1-1½ in. long with a round, flattened head, a short body and frequently two long 'tails' of eggs, referred to by anglers as 'streamers'. It is a marine parasite and lives on the head, flanks and wrist of the tail of the salmon. After the fish has been in fresh water for a little over a day the organism starts to die and then drops off. Therefore, its presence on a salmon is an indication of freshness from the sea, and an angler, when referring to the fish he has caught, is quick to remark on the presence of sea lice. It is almost a mark of salmon respectability—like the bloom on a plum.

Another parasite, which lives on the gills of kelts and 'previous-spawners', is a white grub-like maggot. It is as disreputable an organism as the closely related sea louse is reputable, but this 'Gollum-like' creature has an interesting life-cycle. The free-swimming young attach themselves to the gills of the salmon as they come in from the sea and eventually take up a sedentary, blood-sucking existence. Some of them remain on the gills after the salmon returns to sea and are still there should the salmon return to spawn for a second time. Their presence is therefore a sign that the fish is either a kelt or a previous spawner. A hallmark, one might say, of second-hand goods.

Man never seems to be satisfied with the animals he has in his country and is always introducing new ones, sometimes with disastrous consequences. Classic examples are the grey squirrel in Great Britain and the rabbit in Australia. The same applies to fish in this respect. Sometimes the introduction can be beneficial, as was the introduction of the brown trout and rainbow trout into New Zealand, where there are no related forms with which to compete; in other cases, as with the common carp in Australia and Canada, introductions can be damaging. Scottish fresh waters harbour two alien species closely related to the salmon, namely the rainbow trout and the North American brook trout. Neither seems to be making its presence felt in an unpleasant way as yet, but a third species, the coho salmon, could become a problem. The coho is one of the five species of Pacific salmon. It has a life history similar to the Atlantic salmon, and for this reason may well compete with it for spawning and nursery areas. As it is more aggressive than the Atlantic salmon it could well be the more successful. There is always the fear, as well, that it could transmit a disease to which our salmon has no resistance. At present the coho exists in Scotland only under conditions of strict quarantine in an experimental fish-rearing unit. However, accidents do happen and the Import of Live Fish (Scotland) Bill recently passed through the House of Lords is designed to restrict the import, keeping and release of live fish and shellfish, and the live eggs and milt of fish and shellfish of certain species.

Another species of Pacific salmon has visited us from time to time. This is the pink, or humpbacked, salmon which was introduced by the Russians into their rivers in the Kola Peninsula. One was taken in Shetland waters and two or three have been caught in east-coast estuaries. Fortunately, none has been found in our rivers. It is to be hoped that common sense, and Nature, will prevail and that our own Atlantic salmon will be left to spawn in peace.

Man's attitude to waste-disposal is generally one of 'out of sight, out of mind', and the easiest way of getting waste out of sight is to get it into water, where it will just 'dissolve'. How often we see people throwing refuse into the sea from harbour piers or pleasure craft in the belief that it will vanish, only to find it planted firmly back on the beach at the next high tide. It would be nice if rivers were able to reverse their flow and return highly polluting effluents to those who irresponsibly discharge them into the otherwise pure waters which are our heritage.

A number of rivers in the Central Belt have had their salmon stocks reduced or wiped out by pollution. The Clyde was one of the first to see its salmon go (although they still remain on Glasgow's coat of arms) when the estuary became a cess-pool prohibiting their ascent. No longer can salmon be seen leaping at the ever-impassable Stoneybyres Linn, as described by Colonel Thornton in his *Sporting Tour* (1804). In the last century the waters of the Tweed, the Nith, the Irvine and the Carron were polluted with waste from tweed mills, tanneries, collieries, iron-works and the like, and whereas the Tweed, Nith and Irvine have been restored to their natural purity, the Carron continues to discharge lifeless waters into the Forth. Other rivers, too, have had their problems; in Aberdeen the Don still receives highly oxygen-demanding paper-mill effluent, the decay of which is advertised by a sulphurous odour emanating from the lower reaches near the peaceful Brig o' Balgownie and the austere Bridge of Don. Sewage wastes and mine-water also continue to foul our rivers, but full marks to the whisky distillers who, instead of discharging their highly polluting pot ale into Highland rivers, now process it into animal feedstuffs.

It is not surprising that Scotland, with its mountainous terrain and high rainfall, has harnessed many of its rivers to generate electricity. The majority of the hydro-electric schemes were developed from the late 1940s onwards, following the Hydro-Electric Development (Scotland) Act, 1943. Prior to then there had been limited development in the Tummel-Garry and Conon basins by the Grampian Electricity Supply Company, although the first public supply of electricity in Scotland from a water source came from a water turbine installed in 1890 near the St Benedictine Abbey in Fort Augustus by the abbot.

There are about twenty-five hydro-electric schemes in Scotland at the present time, controlled by the North of Scotland Hydro-Electric Board and the South of Scotland Electricity Board. It is unavoidable that such schemes have adverse effects on migratory fish. The construction of dams prevents the free passage of ascending and descending fish, the formation of reservoirs results in the flooding out of spawning and nursery areas, and rapid changes in river flow, as a result of power-station generation, affect the upstream movement of returning salmon. In addition, the accidental entry of smolts into the turbines of some power stations may lead to a high mortality.

Considerable efforts have been made, by the North of Scotland Hydro-Electric Board in particular, to alleviate these effects. Fish-passes have been built in many of the dams to allow the free movement of fish in both directions. The most famous fish-pass is the one at Pitlochry, where countless tourists come to watch through the observation chamber the fish ascending. The Pitlochry pass (see page 58) is known as a pool-pass, which consists of a series of pools built in such a way that the rise from below the dam to above it is broken up into a number of 'steps' which can be negotiated by salmon and sea trout by either swimming or jumping. Pool-passes are of two general types: one where the water passes from one pool to the next by falling over a weir; the other where the water passes through an orifice in the bottom of the dividing wall between two pools. Pool-passes are relatively expensive to build and, owing to site conditions, may present design difficulties in relation to the main dam structure. A pass working on the principle of a canal lock—designed by a Mr Borland—is now in use in many dams in Scotland. The Borland Pass consists of two pools, one totally enclosed at river level at the foot of the dam and the other at the level of the impoundment above. The pools are joined by a sloping pipe located in the dam structure. The fish are attracted into the pool at the foot of the pipe through an inlet which is then closed. As the water continues to pour in from the upper pool, the level rises and the fish rise with it until they reach the top level; they then jump or swim over the sluice into the reservoir. A number of these passes have observation windows incorporated into the side of the top pool and are a great attraction to visitors, particularly those at Torr Achilty Dam on the River Conon near Strathpeffer, and at the Aigas and Kilmorack Dams on the River Beauly near Inverness.

To compensate for the loss of spawning grounds the North of Scotland Hydro-Electric Board has opened up waters previously inaccessible to salmon by installing fish-passes in insurmountable falls and planting the areas above with salmon eggs and fry from hatcheries located at Invergarry, Contin and Pitlochry Dam. Eggs and fry for the hatcheries come from the Board's traps on the Inverness-shire River Garry at Poulary, the Moriston at Ceannacroc and the Blackwater at Loch na Croic, and in the autumn it is possible to see fishery board staff catching and stripping salmon at these traps.

Another cause for concern is the domestic and industrial use of water resources. Our need for water increases daily and future demands are well illustrated in *A Measure of Plenty*, a report which the Scottish Development Department published in 1973. There are over fifty water-supply reservoirs in central Scotland, as well as a number of river intakes, and Loch Lomond itself. The effects of water-supply schemes on a salmon river are in some ways more severe than those of hydro-electric plants, because the water is actually being removed. Where the water does return to the river its quality is often greatly changed. In addition, the presence of large reservoirs in the upper reaches of salmon rivers inevitably means some reduction in the flow, for the life-restoring flood-waters following a period of drought are held back behind dams. The provision of compensation flows and artificial floods has to be agreed between the salmon district fishery boards and the water services divisions of the regional councils to ensure that there is an adequate volume to allow the unhindered ascent of the salmon and to keep the river environment healthy.

Large tracts of once bare hillside and moorland, forever changing colour and reflecting the mood of sky and cloud, are gradually losing their natural beauty and assuming a

Salmon in the fish-pass at Pitlochry power station

monotonous uniformity as they become clad with ranks of Sitka spruce and larch. As more and more hillsides come under the Forestry Commission plough, there is a detrimental effect on the salmon's environment. Rainstorms bring down silt and gravel from the deeply dug furrows and drains, with the result that water levels in the burns and streams rise quickly producing flash-floods of too short duration and, when the rain stops, drop as fast. The bed-load of gravel is deposited in pools frequented by salmon, making them shallow and uninviting, and the silt smothers the redds and the eggs and alevins beneath.

The effects of drainage schemes were noted by Scrope only a short time before the Land Drainage Acts of 1846 came into force:

'The hills are now so well-drained, that the flood runs off rapidly; and thus the river soon falls in, and becomes too low for the fly, except in the strong streams. Before these complete drainings took place, the Tweed kept full a much longer time than it does at present; for the rains which fell remained in the mosses, which gave out water gradually, like a sponge. Now the hills are scored with innumerable little drains, which empty themselves into the burns, which burns soon become impetuous torrents. . . .'

Some hydrologists would take issue with him, but not all the observations of the many salmon proprietors can be incorrect, and it is clear that the forestry and fishery interests must co-operate to alleviate the deleterious effects of land drainage.

The salmon has been lent a helping hand in its struggle for survival by many interested parties, including proprietors of salmon rivers, salmon district fishery boards and angling associations, as well as the North of Scotland Hydro-Electric Board which, though criticised by many, has spent millions of pounds on fish-passes, traps and hatcheries to guarantee the continuance of salmon stocks in rivers which have been harnessed for power.

An interesting experiment to maintain salmon stocks was carried out on the Conon River system in Ross-shire by myself and Mr Peter Shackley of the Freshwater Fisheries Laboratory at Pitlochry when we were working at the Salmon Research Laboratory in Contin. It was found that the smolts in the River Bran, a tributary of the Conon, were not getting downstream in any numbers as a result of predation by pike, trout and birds and also because of delays while passing through the chain of lochs, reservoirs and dams along the course of the river system. We decided to trap the smolts as they were moving down the River Bran, to transport them by road and to return them to the river downstream of the lowest dam. Over four years we transported 10,500 smolts, 4,700 of which we tagged. The results were beyond our expectations; of those we tagged 168 were recaptured as adult fish. Of the smolts we tagged which used the normal route, none was recaptured as an adult fish.

This is just one illustration of the novel ways which are devised to help the salmon survive.

Salmon are becoming domesticated. They have been reared in hatcheries for decades, but usually only up to the smolt stage. However, in the 1960s, through the efforts of Herr Vik at Sykkylven Fjord, the Norwegians made a breakthrough and started to rear salmon up to the adult stage in cages moored in the enclosed waters of fjords. Soon some well-known British concerns began to show an interest in the process. Scotland now has at least three farms rearing salmon in cages in the sheltered lochs of the west coast. Marine Harvest Ltd, a subsidiary of Unilever, has been sending salmon to Billingsgate Market for some years from its farm at Lochailort. The same firm has recently established salmon farms in Skye and near Ballachulish. In South Uist, Booker McConnell run a salmon farm known as Highland Trout, and Joseph Johnston & Son of Montrose, have an up-and-coming farm at Badcall near Scourie in Sutherland.

Marine Harvest cage-reared salmon being packed for export

'Broiler' salmon are not to everyone's taste; they have pale flesh, and their skins are heavily spotted, tending towards the appearance of a large sea trout.

Be that as it may, broiler salmon are reaching the markets in ever-increasing numbers. I am told that in the spring of 1978 there was a glut of them, the result of which was that the price of 'wild' salmon fell overnight from £2·50 to £1·50 a pound. If the price of wild salmon continues to be affected in this way, it could be argued that they will be less sought after by poachers and some of the pressure will then be taken off the fish. This is all very well, but a price reduction is not necessarily in the best interests of estate and fishery owners, nor of salmon anglers who rely on a good price for their catch so as to pay their rents. There is no doubt, though, that salmon farming has a promising future.

Some authorities hold the view that it is more economical to rear young salmon up to the smolt stage and then allow them to go to sea to feed, relying on their homing instinct to bring them back to the river in which they were released. In this way, they maintain, one obtains a better product. The practice has been in operation for many years, but at first the quality of hatchery-reared smolt did not result in a good return. Smolt-rearing techniques have now improved and the practice now goes under the fashionable term of 'ocean ranching'. A great deal of valuable work in this field is being carried out by the staff of the Freshwater Fisheries Laboratory at their salmon-rearing station at Almondbank near Perth. However, if ocean ranching is to operate on a large scale, the problem will revolve around who is to pay for the production of the thousands of smolts needed to make the exercise an economic one, for the sower of the seed may not be the reaper of the harvest.

The means for ensuring the salmon's survival are therefore available, but whether they will be successful depends on many issues outwith the control of any single body; the final verdict probably lies with the legislator and the politician.

In Perpetuity

THE salmon is an important natural resource which provides a significant contribution to the Scottish economy, and it would be a sad loss to our heritage if it was allowed to dwindle away through bad management. As long ago as 1864 Alexander Russel, editor of *The Scotsman*, warned of the decline in his book *The Salmon*. Many of the reasons for his warning have been described in the previous chapter. Suffice it to say that the writing was already on the wall well over a hundred years ago.

Conservation is in many people's minds and it is important to appreciate what is meant by the term, particularly when referring to an animal which constitutes a natural resource for man's use as opposed to a species which requires protection for its own sake. Dr W. J. Eggeling, one-time Director of the Nature Conservancy (Scotland) (now the Nature Conservancy Council), defined conservation thus:

> 'Conservation basically implies looking after and making the best possible use of a resource, and particularly of a renewable resource—that is, something which through suitable management can produce a yield in perpetuity. Conservation must of necessity involve both fundamental research on all the many resources concerned and conservation research on the intelligent manipulation. Further, conservation seeks the positive information to say: "Do this, do that, manage it thus, conserve it so, make use of it wisely for man."'

The late President John F. Kennedy in his State of the Union message to Congress in 1962 had this to say of conservation:

> 'The wise use of our natural environment, it is in the final analysis the highest form of national thrift—the pre-

vention of wastes and despoilment while preserving, improving and renewing the quality and usefulness of our resources.'

For over 800 years Scotland has endeavoured to protect her salmon stocks by various forms of legislation. In the times of David I (1124-1153) and William the Lyon (1165-1214) it was enacted that in dam dykes there should be a gap big enough in which to allow a three-year-old swine, well fed, to stand. Old Scottish Acts refer to the preservation of 'the reid fische' by means of a close time; to the removal of all standing obstructions to the run of fish, whether meant to capture, or fitted only to impede; and to the measure, weights, prices and other conditions of sale. No better reasons can be given for stopping unseasonable fishing and the use of such fixed engines as traps and fish-weirs than those which occur over and over again in the Scottish statutes of 500 years ago—such practices 'destroy the breed of fish, and hurt the common profit of the realm'. The vigour of these old statutes is as remarkable as their number. For instance, an Act of the First Parliament of James I dated 26th May 1424 runs thus:

'Whosoever be convicted of slaughter of salmon, in time forbidden by the law, shall pay forty shillings for the unlaw, and at the third time if he be convicted of such trespass, he shall lose his life, or pay for it.'

In the early statutes there was provision for fixed engines—more commonly known as cruives—to be done away with in the tidal parts of rivers. Cruives in fresh waters, although they are held by special charter, have now been given up since this method of fishing is detrimental to the proper ascent and distribution of fish, and materially interferes with the value of the neighbouring fisheries. (A well-preserved example of one of these is situated on the River Beauly near Beaufort Castle.)

The three main provisions of the early Scottish Salmon

Acts were thoroughly sound. By the clearance of fixed engines from the estuaries fish were able to enter the rivers unhindered; gaps in fixed engines in fresh waters allowed fish to distribute themselves over the higher reaches, this being assisted also by the operation of a weekly close time; and the wisdom of protecting fish from all fishing during the breeding season was exemplified by the operation of an annual close time.

With the increased awareness of the hazards to salmon stocks, a number of Salmon Acts were passed in the nineteenth century. These included Home Drummond's Act in 1828, which altered the length of the close season; the Tweed Fisheries Acts of 1857 and 1859, which suppressed the use of stell nets and cairn nets, and abolished leistering; the Salmon Fisheries (Scotland) Acts of 1862 and 1868, which set up district fishery boards; and the Solway Salmon Fisheries Commissioners (Scotland) Act of 1877, which abolished the use of certain fixed engines on the Scottish side of the Solway. The Acts of 1862 and 1868 were the most important in that they set up fishery districts and salmon district fishery boards to regulate local matters. The boards are composed entirely of proprietors who hold rights to salmon fishing. The maximum number on any board is seven, and the proprietor with the highest assessed rental acts as chairman. By the Act of 1868 the powers and duties of district boards were defined and extended. Power was given to them to purchase dam dykes, cruives and other fixed engines, for the purpose of removal; to remove any natural obstruction or waterfall by agreement and to attach fish-passes to these; and generally to carry out any work which they consider necessary for the protection and improvement of the fisheries under their charge.

At the time of these Acts industrial development was proceeding at such a pace that serious damage was often caused to salmon stocks before appropriate legislation was available. This applied particularly to pollution, and many rivers in the Central Belt lost their salmon. Archibald

Young, Commissioner of Scottish Salmon Fisheries in the 1870s, reported that in the Forth District the rivers Almond, Avon, Carron, Devon, Esk and Leven were salmonless. Other rivers which suffered badly included the Ayr, Doon, Irvine, Nith and Tweed, the last having ninety-three mills and factories along its banks and along those of its tributaries.

One of the first pollution-prevention Acts, passed by King James VI in 1606, was a statute against the people of Scotland polluting lochs and running streams:

'Our Sovereign Lord and the Estates of Parliament, finding that the laying of lint [flax] in Lochs and Burnes, is not only hurtful to Fishes bred within the same, and Bestial that drinks thereof; but also the hail waters of the said Lochs and Burnes, thereby being infected, is made altogether unprofitable for the use of man, and very noisome to all people dwelling thereabout. Therefore Statutes and Ordains that no person or persons in time coming, lay in Lochs and running Burnes, any green lint, under the pain of Forty Shillings.'

Later there was the Scotch Removal of Nuisances Act of 1856 which imposed a penalty on anyone who discharged into streams any effluent produced in the manufacture of gas, naphtha, vitriol and dye-stuffs. The Act which did the most to control pollution was the Salmon Fisheries (Scotland) Act of 1862 in which it was enacted that:

'Every Person who causes or knowingly permits to flow, or puts or knowingly permits to be put, into any River containing Salmon, any liquid or solid Matter poisonous or deleterious to Salmon, or who shall discharge into any River sawdust to an extent injurious to any Salmon Fishery, shall be liable. . . .'

The Act did much to alleviate the polluted state of the Tweed, which is now an exceptionally clean river.

With the advent of the Rivers (Prevention of Pollution) (Scotland) Acts of 1951 and 1965 and the Control of Pollution Act, 1974, we were able to leave the welfare of our Scottish rivers in the capable hands of the River Purification Boards and the dedicated committee of the Scottish Branch of the Anglers' Co-operative Association, which was set up to fight pollution and help angling clubs in legal actions.

It might have been possible at one time to have said the same for our salmon fisheries because, with the Freshwater Fisheries (Protection) (Scotland) Act, 1951, the legislation was effectively tightened up. It laid down methods of fishing in inland waters (that is, by rod and line, and net and coble); prohibited the use of explosives and poisons, and the taking of dead salmon and trout; and set out the legal procedure for convictions under the Act. It also empowered the Secretary of State for Scotland to collect salmon and sea trout statistics for the purpose of protecting and developing stocks of salmon, although there are limitations on his power to publish the statistics collected.

However, in the early 1960s two problems arose almost simultaneously for which there was no adequate legislation, for the salmon was affected while it was at sea. Until shortly before that time, little was known of the movements and distribution of the salmon. No one had foreseen that the salmon at sea could be at a vulnerable stage of its life-cycle. One of the problems was caused by the starting up in 1958 of a salmon fishery off the west coast of Greenland in which Scottish salmon were caught; the other was inshore drift-netting for salmon off the east coast of Scotland. The latter was soon dealt with, albeit temporarily. Section 7 of the Sea Fish Industry Act, 1959, as amended, gave the Minister for Agriculture and Fisheries powers to make orders prohibiting fishing for salmon and migratory trout in any area within or outside territorial waters adjacent to Great Britain, although the methods of fishing that are prohibited must be stated in the order. Section 2 of the White Fish and Herring Industries Act, 1948, was amended in 1962 to give the Minister power to prohibit fishing for salmon and migratory trout in any part of the sea specified in the appropriate order, except under licence. (Nigel Tranter wrote an amusing story at this time, based on the illegal netting off the Berwickshire coast. Called *Kettle of Fish*, it is well worth reading as long as one does not take it too seriously. It is also, once more, a topical subject.) At the same time as a ban was put on drift-net fishing off the Scottish coast the Secretary of State for Scotland set up a committee under the chairmanship of Lord Hunter 'to review the law relating to salmon and trout fisheries in Scotland, including the Tweed, and its operation . . . and to recommend such changes in the law as might be thought desirable'.

The Hunter Committee produced two reports by 1965, but eleven years passed before any of the proposals were implemented and then only one of them, the statutory protection of brown trout, was incorporated into the Freshwater and Salmon Fisheries (Scotland) Act, 1976.

The Greenland salmon fishery developed at an incredible speed. In 1958 the catch from the inshore hang-nets was two metric tons; in 1964 it was 1,539 tons. An offshore fishery was established in 1966, and in 1969 the total catch from the inshore and offshore fisheries was 2,210 tons, exceeding the total annual Scottish salmon catch. The recovery in Greenland waters of salmon tagged in Scottish rivers as smolts has caused growing concern for the future of Scottish salmon stocks.

In the late 1960s the major salmon-producing countries were seriously concerned by the rapid expansion of this fishery. There were demands for action, and in 1969, following an international conference called by the Atlantic Salmon Research Trust and the International Atlantic Salmon Foundation, the International Commission for the Northwest Atlantic Fisheries adopted a resolution recommending a complete ban on fishing for salmon throughout the convention area. This was aimed directly at stopping high-seas fishing off west Greenland, but because of formal objection to the resolution by West Germany (on a matter of principle) and by Denmark and Norway (the major participants in the fishery) it was rendered null and void. However, at the I.C.N.A.F. meeting in 1970 countries objecting to the resolution agreed to curtail fishing to the four months from 1st August to 30th November, not to exceed the level of the 1969 catch and the number of fishing vessels engaged, and to forgo the use of pelagic trawls and monofilament nets, except for certain specified Danish boats already equipped with the latter. Additionally, West Germany agreed to refrain from fishing off Greenland.

The breakthrough came with the United States—Denmark agreement in 1972 following the passage of a Bill in the United States aimed at Denmark and giving power to prohibit the importation into the United States of fish products from any country deemed to be fishing against the dictates of 'conservation'. At the 1972 annual meeting of I.C.N.A.F. it was finally agreed, without objection, that all fishing for salmon outside Greenland's national fishery limits (twelve miles) would cease after 1st January 1976; that in the intervening years the catch taken by Danish vessels, including Faroese, by Norway, and by other countries fishing off Greenland, would be progressively reduced; and that for future years the annual catch taken by local Greenland fishermen would be limited to 1,100 metric tons.

However, there was no time for Scotland to become complacent, because no sooner had the problem of the Greenland fishery been resolved than illegal inshore drift-net fishing around the Scottish coast started up again. Scottish inshore seine-net fishermen argued that if the English could drift-net for salmon off the Northumberland coast, why could they not do the same, particularly as it was likely that the English fishermen were taking salmon destined for Scottish rivers? Even though effective legislation was available with the Sea Fish (Conservation) Act of 1967 and the Statutory Instrument Orders of 1972 and 1975, made through the Act to counteract loopholes in the original wording, and to ban the landing of salmon, there were flagrant acts of 'piracy' and outright defiance of the law. On one occasion, in 1976, a skipper of a boat illegally drift-netting for salmon off Montrose, on being boarded at sea by the police and officials of the local district fishery board, refused to return to port and, disobeying police orders, headed for the open sea. There have been a number of cases of boats attempting to ram vessels belonging to the district boards; but perhaps the most serious incident occurred in 1977 when a patrol launch belonging to the River Tweed Commissioners was sunk while anchored in Berwick Harbour—a deed which smacks of a return to the state of affairs existing in Berwick over 100 years ago. In a notice entitled 'Instructions for the Guidance of Bailiffs on Board the Steamboat employed by the Tweed Commissioners' and signed 'By Order of the Commissioners, Steph. Sanderson, Clerk for the Lower District, Berwick, 11th Sept, 1861' (see page 71), one of the instructions states that 'Should the steamer be attacked with stones or otherwise, and should there be any reason to believe that the attack will be continued, two of the crew should be immediately sent ashore . . . to report the matter to the Borough Police'.

Illegal drift-netting continues on the pretence of fishing for mackerel or dogfish, and although with the help of helicopters and fishery cruisers arrests have been made and convictions obtained, the resultant fines have been no deterrent. In some cases the charges were brought under the 1951 Act for which the maximum fine was a mere £150, while others were made under the Salmon Fisheries Act of 1976 in which the penalties are more severe. Fiscals have been notified that fines of up to £50,000 can be imposed under the Fisheries Limits Act of 1976. However, the problem of enforcement remains, and one solution, which is supported by the Association of Scottish District Salmon Fishery Boards and the Salmon and Trout Association, may stem from a Private Member's Bill, the Sale of Salmon Bill, which was introduced in the House of Commons on 3rd February 1978. It is designed to prohibit the sale of salmon taken and

INSTRUCTIONS FOR THE
GUIDANCE OF BAILIFFS
ON BOARD THE STEAMBOAT
EMPLOYED BY THE
TWEED COMMISSIONERS.

1. The Boat shall have her Steam up half-an-hour before Sunset every Night, and at other times as required by the Superintendent.

2. The Crew shall consist of 6 Bailiffs, including the Steersman, but exclusive of Engineman and Stoker, all of whom shall live on board the Boat. The Superintendent will regulate the Leave on Shore, but so as no more than Two Men shall be ashore at one Time.

3. There shall at all times, both by Night and Day, be at least Two Men on Deck keeping a Look-out.

4. During Daylight the Steamer shall be Moored opposite Hallow Stell, as close to the Shore as possible, so as to command all that goes on at Spittal. It will be particularly desirable for the Steamer to be Moored, so as to enable the Bailiffs to see the Boats as they come in from the White Fishing, as thus the Faces of the Fishermen will become familiar; but the Steamer must not be placed so as needlesly to be in the way of the Fishermen landing their Boats. While the Tide is suitable for Fishing during the Night the Boat shall be kept constantly moving up and down the River, from Sanstell Point to the Carr Rock or thereabouts, and on no account shall be removed from the Station. While in motion, the Grappling Irons shall be kept constantly out, and a supply of Lights shall be kept on board. When the Tide does not suit for Fishing after Sunset the Boat must be Moored at the Lower Buoy near the Carr Rock, or as much nearer Spittal as possible, so as to command a View of the Shore.

5. The Steamer shall on no account come up to Berwick Quay except to take in Coals, or by the express order of the Clerk to the Commissioners. The Small Boat shall be used to Land any of the Crew coming on Shore.

6. Every endeavour must be used to identify Persons infringing the law. If a Person is found engaged in Illegal Fishing he may be at once taken into custody and detained till the Morning, when he may be brought before a Magistrate—Boats engaged in Illegal Fishing, as well as nets may be seized.

7. It is the strict order of the Commissioners that their Bailiffs shall not needlesly come into personal collision with the inhabitants of Spittal or elsewhere. If Illegal Fishing is going on it will be the duty of the Bailiffs, notwithstanding any attempt at opposition, to detect and identify the offenders, and to seize the Boats and Nets engaged; but if the Offenders cannot be at once apprehended without causing a riot, it will be sufficient to identify them and report their Names to the Superintendent, so as they may be prosecuted in regular course. The Bailiffs are particularly warned not to be provoked, under any circumstances, to use irritating expressions to any person whomsoever, but to observe perfect quietness while on duty.

8. Should the Steamer be attacked with stones or otherwise, and should there be reason to believe that the attack will be continued, Two of the Crew should be immediately sent ashore in the Small Boat, one to remain with the Boat and the other to report the matter to the Superintendent of the Borough Police; but it must be clearly understood that the Commissioners only sanction an application to the Borough Police in cases where stones are thrown or other violence used against the Bailiffs or the Steamer. The Police are only to be called in to aid and protect persons and property from injury. Any attack upon the Bailiffs or the Steamer must also be reported early the next morning to the Superintendent and by him to the Clerk to the Commissioners.

9. As the Crew will be thoroughly protected by Nettings from Stones, it is expected that the Boat shall not be withdrawn merely in consequence of attacks from the Shore. If she is kept steadily on the move so as to prevent Nets being Fished, the principal object will be attained, and the people on the Shore must sooner or later tire of calling up and down to throw Stones if they see that no attention is paid to them.

10. The Superintendent will give orders when the Steamer shall go to sea to look after Bob Nets set there.

11. The Superintendent will also give Orders for the Crew to act on Shore when necessary, but if at Night Two of the Crew must be left on board the Steamer. While on Shore, Bailiffs are warned to keep together unless ordered to the contrary. They must obey the Commands of their Leader, and, as far as possible, keep silence. They must on no account use taunting expressions or gestures, and they are only justified in using their Staves in Self-defence.

12. A regular Log shall be kept on board, and a Copy left every Morning with the Clerk to the Commissioners.

By Order of the Commissioners.
STEPH. SANDERSON,
Clerk for the Lower District.

Berwick, 11th Sept., 1861.

PRINTED AT THE ADVERTISER OFFICE, BERWICK.

acquired illegally. Unfortunately the Bill was talked out and went to the bottom of the legislative pile and must now await reintroduction.

It is to be hoped that most M.Ps have a greater sense of responsibility than was shown by one of their members, Mr William Hamilton, who said:

'One of the most honourable professions in the Highlands of Scotland is that of the poacher. I do not believe that he is thieving at all. The thieving went on at a much earlier date, and the poachers are taking something that is their right'—(*Hansard*, Friday, 3rd February 1978).

Our endeavours to conserve salmon stocks for posterity continue. Organisations strive for better legislation and biologists, fishermen and administrators meet at conferences and symposia to discuss and make resolutions. Because the greatest threat to our salmon may be on the high seas, the Law of the Sea Conference may be the place to draw attention to this. Vice-Admiral Sir Hugh Mackenzie, Director of the Atlantic Salmon Research Trust, had this to say:

'The Law of the Sea Conference continues: it covers a daunting number of subjects and has an equally daunting number of participants, the vast majority of whom have no connection with salmon. Nevertheless, progress has been made along the lines jointly supported by the major salmon-producing countries of the North Atlantic, and at the end of the last session in mid-1975 a draft text of an Article [Draft Article 54] specifying measures for the conservation of salmon had been produced; it is to be hoped that endorsement of this Article will be obtained at future sessions of the Conference.'

The future of the salmon is in our hands. We must make sure that our grandchildren will be able to stare through fishmongers' windows and read the label proclaiming one of Scotland's most valuable natural assets—Scotch Salmon.